Edith Carr
Life on Malham Moor

When the summer sun is shining
   And the sky is brightest blue;
The flowers and the pastures
   Are in their deepest hue.
But when the snow comes whistling
   And winds rattle every door –
Spare a thought for those who live
   Upon this cold, bare Moor.

Edith Carr

Edith Carr (signature)

Edith Carr
Life on Malham Moor

by **W. R. Mitchell**

CASTLEBERG
1999

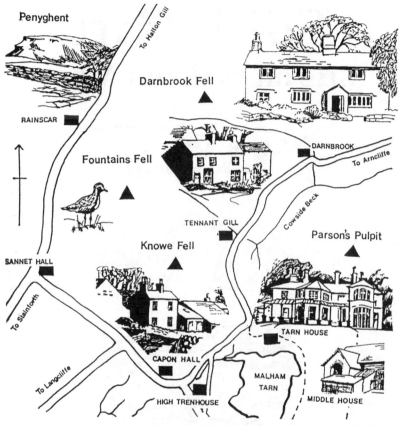

Drawn by Margaret Blackburne.

A **Castleberg** Book.

First published in the United Kingdom in 1999.

Text © W R Mitchell 1999.

The moral right of the author has been asserted.

ISBN 1 871064 67 8

Typeset in Palatino, printed and bound in the United Kingdom by Lamberts Print & Design, Station Road, Settle, North Yorkshire, BD24 9AA.

Published by Castleberg, 18 Yealand Avenue, Giggleswick, Settle, North Yorkshire, BD24 0AY.

Introduction

I FIRST MET Edith many years ago when Granada Television were preparing a documentary based on *The Dalesman* magazine, which I had the good fortune to edit. I was asked to tour the district, chatting with interesting people. Edith had come to my notice as the writer of evocative verse based on her experiences at a remote farm on Malham Moor.

She was then living with her husband, Robert, in a small cottage at Langcliffe. Sitting in a corner of her living room, she recited a poem about Capon Hall, locally known as Capna', and we then visited the place for filmed sequences that would match the words. An old gate obliged by squeaking as it moved on its rusty hinges.

Subsequently, I tape-recorded Edith as she recalled life at a storm-wracked farm on Malham Moor. Having bought a camcorder, I filmed her as shepherdess, in charge of half a dozen sheep reared as pet lambs. They were quartered at the remnants of a little farm near her home. Standing at the door of her barn, Edith could see the limestone hill on which the ashes of Robert, her husband, had been scattered. His family knew the end was near when he stopped asking about the sheep.

In her modest farming enterprise near Craven Quarry at Langcliffe, Edith wore a woollen cap that had belonged to Robert. She claimed it brought her luck. The sheep had lost their natural timidity and were strong enough to cause injury when Edith appeared with a bucket containing special rations. She was persuaded to part with the sheep. One evening I filmed the negotiations between her and a family friend, John Mellin, who arrived to bid for them.

In truth, Edith and John had haggled in private. They had fixed a scale of prices before the camera was brought into use. You would not have guessed it from the protracted way in which haggling was resumed. The end of the bargaining came in the traditional way – with a cordial slapping of hands.

Edith now devoted her considerable energies towards her most unusual garden. The plants were rooted in dozens of metal containers of various sizes that were set on the flags before her cottage home. So profuse was the growth that the containers vanished from sight.

Hanging from a wall was the skull of a tup, with huge curving horns. Edith and one of her daughters had found it while walking on the hills. With a shiver of excitement, they noticed the horn burn was RC, for Robert Carr. This tup was one owned by Edith and her husband. They named it Rastus. It was "a bad old thing" prone to charge humans. Rastus, when about five-shear, had wandered off in the Great Snow of 1947, over 40 years before. The family had often wondered about its fate.

During spells of videoing, both at her home and at Capon Hall on Malham Moor, I got to know Edith's life story well. Her father had been killed on active service in the 1914-18 war. Mother died during the 'flu epidemic towards the end of that war. Edith was raised by grandparents who were farmers. The last phase of her education was at Skipton Girls'

High School. Her first job, early in the 1939-45 war, was in the Women's Land Army, allocated to her family's farm at Hanlith in Malhamdale.

Edith married Robert Carr, a native of Malham Moor who took the first opportunity of tenanting one of the hill farms. For almost a quarter of a century, at Capon Hall, or Capna' as it shall henceforth be known, Edith was wife, mother, dairymaid and general labourer. Here she bore four children – Anne, Robin, Mary and Stephen - who grew up fit and healthy. Here she rejoiced in good days and at other times battled with Nature at her meanest.

On the staff at Capna' were collie dogs, including Laddie and Bess. Another fine sheepdog, Bonzo, was allowed to live on in retirement when his active days were over. He walked round and round, as though gathering sheep. One morning, he was nowhere to be found. It was presumed he had wandered to some quiet spot to die.

The Malham Moor days covered a period of rapid social and farming changes. The legendary Walter Morrison, who called Malham Tarn House "my mountain home," had died some twenty years earlier but Edith was to remember the Ushers, gamekeeper and wife, and especially Mrs Usher for she was rarely known to leave her moorland home. Old Mr Winskill, the agent, who married a member of the Coates family, was still well remembered by the denizens of Malham Moor.

What had been an isolated and thinly spread community acquired mobility through the motor car and, with the coming of electricity in the 1950s, a ready link with the outside world through the telephone. When they first attended church at Kirkby Malham they "made downbank," travelling in a float drawn by a horse named Bob and taking a good half hour over the journey. On the return journey, Robert invariably walked, using the long reins to control Bob. He felt that his great weight, added to that of the children, would be too much for the old horse. Eventually, they had a car, which made churchgoing much easier.

Edith remembers when they visited Laycocks at Skipton for "winter-dip," a greasy concoction that was added to the sheep dip and left a form of insulation on skin and wool. Almost every farm had a goat, which produced a kid early enough in the year for there to be a good flow of milk by the time the hill sheep were lambing. In her young days at Winterburn a simple task like feeding free-range hens was fraught with danger if the billy-goat was about. It was as adroit as Edith at scaling fences. On Malham Moor, the goat was in effect a mobile milk bar, with the milk kept at just the right temperature to be of use to weakly lambs in need of extra nourishment. Edith would take Nanny, the goat, into the barn to give the lamb a warm drink. A bad-tempered billy-goat associated with the farm came and went as it pleased and was last seen on Craven Rocks, above Langcliffe.

Everyone growing up on a farm in the days before cattle were subject to artificial insemination will have a tale to tell of a close encounter with a bull. Edith tells of a "mad cow...it was worse than a bull, especially when there was a woman in sight. It would go for her." A near neighbour who had not mentioned its aggressive nature had sold the cow to the Carrs. The cow was despatched to the abattoir.

Edith and Robert Carr, moving to Capna' in the 1940s, were thrown back on their own resources. Edith might not leave the farm for months at a time. Her husband did the shopping on his periodic trips to the auction mart. The winters were almost unbearably long, inducing some hill farmers to "sup ale" to excess at the nearest hostelry. There were no licensed premises on the moor itself.

The tale is told of two Dales farmers who went to a tup fair, bought an animal and then repaired to an inn, where they spent freely. When they emerged, they could not decide which was the tup they had bought and they picked a likely one, which proved to be one of the best. What should they do about it? They had it slaughtered and both families ate it.

On Malham Moor, the relatively few families "got on" with each other. With cattle and sheep widely spread across the landscape, honesty was vital. So was mutual help, a feature of such annual tasks as sheep-clipping. In the pre-electricity age, candles flickered in the bedroom and paraffin lamps burned in living room and kitchen. The so-called hurricane lamp hung in the shippon at milking time in winter and was carried around the lambing crofts in springtime.

Some of the remedies used for ailing stock might be classified as "black magic" but others worked. A case in point was rowelling a cow which, while being wintered in a shippon, acquired an inflamed joint on a front leg that bore the weight of the animal as it rose. Relief was afforded to the animal when the puss had drained away.

Edith explains: "We got a big needle – the sort used for closing up wool-sacks. This needle was threaded with string and a piece of bacon rind was attached. The knee was bathed in hot water and then the needle and string were dipped in salt-and-water, which was the best available antiseptic. The needle enabled the string to be quickly passed through the swollen part of the limb. From the wound came a lot of puss. When the strip of bacon rind was in the wound, it was left there for several days, by which time the wound had been drained of matter. It was a gruesome business but it didn't seem to hurt the cow. And it felt much better when it had been carried out."

I was impressed by Edith's love of Capna', even though it represented much toil and privation. Her researches showed the Great Moor had been peopled for many centuries. In monastic days, Fountains Abbey had vast grazing rights in the Craven district. The abbey gave its name to Fountains Fell, the highest point of what became the parish of

Malham Moor. Edith's vivid imagination peopled the present with folk from the past, such as "holy men and others" who followed the green tracks across the Moor, stopping to pray at the wayside crosses that established the limit of abbey land and were also an early form of way-marking.

Malham Tarn provided the abbey with trout. From the sheep-houses of Malham Moor, the Abbot benefited from mutton and wool, especially wool. Traders from the Continent queued at the abbey to buy wool that was regarded as among the finest available. The goodness of sheep's milk was locked up in cheeses that the abbey could store for use in the lean winter months.

With her farmhouse background, and grandparents who regularly made butter, Edith was familiar with the dairy processes. In olden days, the cheese-making process was started off using the dried stomach of a calf, known as keslop. Later, rennet was employed. Boiled well, then cooled and stirred into the milk at blood-heat, this agent ensured that the curds would form.

Edith had a particular fascination for the period when cattle from Scotland – the vulgar [black] cattle of the Highlands and Islands – were driven south to help to meet the need for beef from inhabitants of the fast-growing towns of England. Such cattle were also known in the northern dale-country as "kyloes" because initially they had to swim the kyles from the islands to the mainland.

Edith thought of "wiry Scottish drovers passing Capna with their lean, lank, long-horned cattle, mangy and scraggy after their weeks of walking from the Borders and beyond, through the long miles of the Pennines...They were heading for the Great Close, beyond Malham Tarn, where great sales were held." In much more recent times, Robert's family, who had farmed at Catgill, Bolton Abbey, had regularly visited Scotland to buy cattle, which were driven back into the Dales via Appersett, Hawes, Buckden and Appletreewick. The cattle were rested and then dispersed to farms in the Winterburn and Rylstone areas. The Carrs had farming interests at Winterburn.

Edith has written: "Farmers who travelled along the old road through Wharfedale would, at Thorpe, mingle with farmers from Rylstone, Hetton and Flasby. There must have been gruesome tales told of murder and foul deeds at remote spots like Boss Moor. Such tales would be sparked off by men soaked in ale."

The best-known resident of Capna' was Abraham Banks, the sage of Malham Moor, who died in 1944 at the ripe old age of 85. He farmed at Capon Hall for 57 years. Old Abraham had side whiskers and bore the marks of a hard life spent among the Pennine fells. His mind was a repository of much of the parish lore.

Abraham, like many another, was proud of his Malham Moor connections. Once, whisked off to Leeds Infirmary for an operation, he was lying on the operating table when he overheard a staff nurse say to a doctor: "What a queer old man; I wonder where he comes from." Abraham, not yet knocked out by the anaesthetic, sat up and said: "I'm Abraham Banks; I come from Capna, on Malham Moor. Surely you've heard of Capna'?"

Hearing Edith tell endless tales of the past, I determined to jot down her memories of high life in the Dales. They would be given permanence in a book. Here is the result, which includes Edith's own observations and some of her impressions in verse. The line drawings are the work of Richard Bancroft.

Edith's Story

SHE WAS born in 1918 and never knew her parents. Her father, John Hird, died that same year while serving with the Army in France. Her mother, Alice, as related, fell victim to a virulent form of influenza that ravaged the population towards the end of the Great War. "I was six months old at the time and went to live with my grandparents, who were farmers at Harden, in the Aire Valley."

Grandad, Thomas Shackleton, prided himself on his sheep, which were Lonks, the breed of the Southern Pennines. "They are big sheep with broad backs. The wool is short in the staple and clings tightly to the body. It doesn't drag in snowtime." He had a horse and cart with which he led stone from the sandstone quarries that were squandered about the moor. The stone was needed for building work in the fast-growing industrial town of Keighley.

Granny, who bore the unusual Christian name of Paulina, told Edith about the flu epidemic in which four of her family had died. From Harden, the family moved to The Rookery at Winterburn, in a quiet valley, among the gentle hills of mid-Craven. Here they farmed for 12 years. Edith, as a girl, attended Gargrave National School, which involved a walk of four miles each way.

Mr Deadman, the headmaster, asked Edith to deliver a message concerning church matters to Mrs Wills at the palatial Eshton Hall. She felt very important as she opened the big iron gates at the bottom of the drive and walked between the yew trees, across the lawns and up to the large front door. A butler in a black-fitted jacket opened the door and took the slip of paper on which the message was written.

"As I waited," Edith recalls, "I saw a polished oak floor, adorned by a huge lion skin and fierce-looking head. The hall had oak beams and, to the right, a cage of colourful birds." Mrs Wills appeared. She was tall, with silver hair, dressed mostly in grey or blue. After thanking Edith, she gave her some flowers from a big vase on the hall table.

Another of Edith calling points was the splendid Friar's Head, built in the 17th century by a member of the Procter family who had been a monastic agent. Now it was the home of Jim and Minnie Taylor. "Jim was a typical Dales farmer, wearing fustian breeches. He was always in his shirt sleeves. Jim wore clogs and, like almost every Dales farmer, was always 'busy', with three or four dogs, attending to the sheep or rounding up cattle."

Minnie Taylor, small and quick, was like Jim, "always on the go." Her dark hair was plaited and rolled at the sides into 'earphones', which was the fashion of the day. Her cheeks were like two rosy apples. She spoke with a Northumbrian accent and told Edith it took her a whole day to clean over 1,000 small panes of glass that were set in the windows at the front of the house.

The Shackletons moved from Winterburn to Hall Farm, Hanlith, in Malhamdale. By this time, Edith was attending Skipton Girls' High School and her daily walk was less arduous. She caught a bus at Drinkall's Corner, near Eshton Hall. George and Wilfred Parker had inaugurated this valuable bus service that would soon be taken over by the up-and-coming *Pennine* company. At Hanlith, one of the Malhamdale villages founded by the Angles, the hall itself was of ancient foundation but had been greatly extended, its gateway adorned by carved halberds, suggesting an association with the Sergeantson family, though it was now the home of Dudley Illingworth and his family.

The cattle at Hall Farm were typical of those being kept in the Dales – Shorthorns, dual purpose animals, excelling at both milk production and, if required, as beefers. Edith, helping to prepare cows for the auction mart, sandpapered their horns, spread red ruddle on their udders and washed and brushed their faces and backs. "How smart they looked as they walked around the ring."

Almost every farm had a pig and in November, when the slaughterer made his rounds, the gruesome task was accomplished and in due course salted pork dangled from hooks in the kitchen ceiling, where it was being left to dry out and mature. Edith hated pig-killing day, when an animal cared for over the months was bound and roped on to the stock, slaughtered, scalded with boiling water from the set-pot and scraped until no bristles remained.

She was an unwilling participant in the rites that followed – the hoisting of the carcass on to a wooden beam, where it was slit open and left to cool; the subsequent ritual of cutting it up into hams, sides of bacon and shoulders. "The head was cut up ready to be salted and made into brawn. The leaves of fat were cut into small pieces that were placed in a pan and set over the fire to be rendered down as lard. This was stored in stone jam jars until it was used on baking day."

It was reckoned that when a pig was killed only its squeal was wasted. Scraps were placed on a meat dish, sprinkled with salt and eaten cold, with toast, and liver was made into savoury ducks, the mixture being composed of the liver, plus onions, sage and rice. The pig's blood, caught in a can and salted, was poured on to a mixture composed of rice, oatmeal, onions, herbs and milk and transformed as black puddings.

Christmas at Granny's was noted for its feel-good factor. "When I came downstairs on Christmas morning, the house would be lovely and warm, a big fire was burning in every grate and the table was laden with good things to eat and presents for all." The Christmas roses that grew by the side of the porch were brought into the living room and displayed in a willow-patterned bowl kept on the sideboard. A bunch of holly was suspended from the ceiling and sprigs of holly were placed along the top of every picture frame.

So much food was eaten that it was a day or two before ribs settled back into place. A lump of ham was boiled and mince pies were baked. Wheat, whisky and elderberry wines were brought out of hiding. (They were kept under the stairs). From other "secret places" came dates and nuts. Red apples and tangerines were on display. Granny made a large Christmas cake that was iced and sprinkled with silver pieces and pink flowers.

When the Christmas lunch was ready to be served, Granny took her oven cloth, opened the oven door, drew out the cooked goose and smiled when the fork came out of the flesh easily. It signified that the bird had been cooked "well enough." The pudding, "brown and gooey," adorned by a piece of holly, was served with sweet sauce, to which a tot of rum had been added.

Christmas enlivened the winter season. "Then it was springtime, with bluebells, pale green beech leaves and pale sunshine. The lambs skipped and played, but woe betide a sick lamb if Mr Crow saw him. He would swoop down, pick out the lamb's eyes and then dismember it. The crows were cruel. I did not like the crows."

When, in 1939, the Second World War broke out, Edith enrolled in the Women's Land Army and was given an opportunity of continuing to help her grandparents at Hall Farm. She had special pleasure in caring for the young stock. "All the local boys were called up for the Army or the Home Guard. Everybody knitted caps, scarves and gloves. All were busy working for the war effort."

Nightly, Edith heard the drone of German bombers passing over the dale on their way to Liverpool. "Then a dull red glow would appear in the sky and we knew they were bombing the docks. How thankful we were to be living in relative peace in Malhamdale."

The Road to Capon Hall

EDITH SHACKLETON and Robert Carr were married at Kirkby Malham church on a dark and dreary first day of March, 1943. The officiating clergyman was the Rev A B Chick, "a real live wire; he was always on the go." On weekdays, he travelled from farm to farm on an ancient Royal Enfield motor bike and when local people saw him pass, with his cassock flapping in the wind, they marvelled that it did not catch in the spokes and throw him off the machine.

Edith had been a regular attender at the "lovely old church," which had been restored by Mr Morrison, of Malham Tarn House. She went to all the services, sang in the choir and admired the stained glass windows if the sermons were dull. She met Robert in 1941 at one of the Home Guard dances held in the Church Hall at Kirkby Malham. Robert, being a Malham Moorer, was a bit bashful. Edith, a bonnie young lady, had flirted with some of the other lads but was also inherently shy. "He plucked up courage and asked me to dance."

Robert, who had lived on Malham Moor since he was fourteen years old, was working for his kinsfolk at Lee Gate, a big sheep farm that was approached on a narrow, wall-bound road from Malham, passing close to Janet's Foss and Gordale Scar. In those days, few farmers had a car and attended social events like dances on push-bikes. It was quite an effort for Robert to meet up with Edith at dances far down the dale. And when the dancing was over, he had the long uphill walk back to Lee Gate.

The courtship had to fit in with life on a dale farm where some of the fields had been "turned brown side up" by the plough. Oats and barley had been planted. Another large field was sown down to turnips, which would provide extra rations for the sheep. "All the fields needed rather more attention than pastures; the growing crops were to be weeded so the hoe was in daily use. The turnips were 'topped' and 'tailed'."

In the Craven district, cereals grew lustily but in the damp climate the ears might rot. If the crop ripened satisfactorily, a "binder" dealt with the oats. The bundles it dropped were set up in batches of eight as stooks. Edith remembers with a wince how her arms came into contact with nettles and thistles. It was left to the wind and sunshine to dry out the stooks. In September, the threshing machine arrived. Sometimes, the work went on all night. Sacks of corn were taken to the granary to be stored and used for winter fodder.

As the day of their marriage approached, Edith and Robert secured the tenancy of a small farm near Austwick. They purchased some sheep and "a few bits of farm tackle." Attending a furniture sale, they bought a bed, a table, two chairs, a rocking chair and a desk – all for £5.

For the wedding, Edith, aged twenty-four, mustered enough clothing coupons to deck herself in a dress of clover pink crepe. A spray of blue iris and pink tulips was worn on the shoulder. Her hat and gloves were brown. The young couple stood in a 15th century church that was dubbed "the cathedral of the Dales." Mrs Illingworth, of Hanlith Hall, had provided floral decorations. Mrs Shearer was the organist. As they left for a family gathering at the local pub, someone took a photograph – one photograph – which scarcely did justice to the occasion.

"We set off by train for a honeymoon in Blackpool. The place was teeming with RAF personnel. We had arranged to stay with some friends of mine. They were a kind old couple and did all they could to make us comfortable in their small bungalow." On their return to the Dales, Edith and Robert assumed the tenancy of Southwaite, a farm at Wharfe, in the parish of Austwick. (The farm name was changed through a clerical error at Lancaster post office as Sowerthwaite).

Sunshine in March offered the promise of an early spring. "We bought a good horse called Bob, though he would never walk; he must always trot. We got a cart, loaded our few belongings – bed, table, chairs, a small amount of food and a sack of coal – and set off for Southwaite." This plain little farm stood near the foot of Crummock Dale, rather more than a bowshot from the hamlet of Wharfe.

The valley, with its outcrops of Silurian rock, was flanked by Long

Scar, an outlier of Ingleborough. Moughton Hill was capped with limestone and had ancient slate foundations. A "clapper" bridge spanned the beck and on either side of the valley was a track, one heading for Crummock Farm and the other offering one way to Horton-in-Ribblesdale. This track ran near a small area where farmers collected whetstone, to be used for sharpening their scythes.

The fact that their farmhouse was small – "two up, two down" – did not worry the newly-married couple. They had few possessions. "We had bought an old wringer and two dolly-tubs, which were set opposite the sink. The ceiling was dark and low. We fixed our bed in the space over the living-room and, not having a wardrobe, put our clothes in boxes and pushed them under the bed." Edith, eyeing with a grimace the drab inner walls, hopped on to a bicycle and visited Settle on market day to buy some Sunshine Yellow paint, which made the walls of their little farm look "nice and bright." When the house had been scrubbed out, she put some net curtains at the windows. Two pots of red geraniums were set on a window-sill.

Having been married in March, Edith and Robert had some good weather ahead. They saw a "bright golden haze on the meadows." They were in a valley tenanted by curlew, snipe, wheatear and lapwing. "Each morning, Robert would milk the cows while I fetched the horse from the pasture. We had six milkers and sent off quite a nice drop of milk to the dairy at Leeds. We also had several heifer calves, which I fed, and a pig and some hens that provided us with bacon and eggs."

It was during the brief tenancy of Southwaite Farm that Edith experienced one of nature's excesses – a whirlwind. She and Robert were well into their first haytime. Sunshine and breezes had turned the mown grass into crisp and sweet-smelling hay. It was now ready to be put into pikes [large weatherproof heaps]. Edith was working in the field when the sky darkened and a vigorous wind developed. The whirlwind took every wisp of hay out of the field. "I saw it whirling the hay up to a great height and we never saw it again. I thought it was going to take me, so I laid down flat."

Their first child, Anne, was born a year after their marriage. Edith still did her outside jobs, keeping an eye on Anne. Baby-watching duties were shared by a young dog named Laddie, which Edith had brought from Hanlith. If a stranger approached, the dog growled and its hair bristled. At times, Edith fancied she could hear footsteps on the passage, even when the flanking doors were locked. Was the house haunted? A neighbour said that two old brothers had spent all their lives at the farm and had died here. "Were they visiting us?"

Edith and Robert were happy at Southwaite. "Then Grandad and Granny Carr told us that Capon Hall Farm, on Malham Moor, was to be let. Grandad thought it would be a good idea to live there. Capon Hall was being offered on lease by John Ingham, of Langcliffe Mill. It had been farmed by a man called Maurice Robinson, who latterly had an ailing wife.

Edith knew Capna' as the home of Abraham Banks, a wise old man who had lived on one of the two farms for over fifty years. The farm would give them an opportunity to improve themselves. Such an opportunity came but once in a lifetime. Robert made an appointment to see John Ingham, who offered him the tenancy.

It was in November that Robert visited Capna' for a chat with Mr Robinson, in the hope that the take-over of tenancy might occur before the onset of winter – a high Pennine winter that seemed to occupy most of the year. Edith recalls: "By this time I was expecting my second child, so I wasn't in a good position for trailing about a lot.

"Mr Robinson, who planned to move to Clapham, was quite willing for us to take the farm and so we paid for the ingoings, such as the hay lying in the barn, and bought some milk cows from him. Robert's tups and yows were moved to Capna'.

"I was expecting my baby to be born on the 11th of November and decided to stay at home rather than go to hospital. It was best to stay at Southwaite for the time being. On the appointed day, Robert had arranged to visit Capna'. I started to be badly. The arrival of the baby was imminent. I was on my own.

"Fortunately, an old woman called Mrs Constantine, who lived down in Wharfe, came up to see me. She'd taken to me, had this old woman.

Mrs Constantine went off and telephoned for the midwife and doctor. The midwife was Mrs Johnson, newly arrived at Paley Green. This was to be the first baby she had delivered since her move. She and the doctor had no sooner got in the house than my baby came – quite a big baby, 8 lb 9 oz. Everything went on all right. When Robert came home he was surprised. I said: 'I'm not going to Capna till he's a week or a fortnight old'. By the end of 10 days I'd got out of bed and started packing..."

Fortunately, being new starters, Edith and Robert did not have much furniture. "The furniture got piled on to our horse-drawn cart. Robert settled me among the bedding on top. I'm sure we looked like gipsies as we set off for Capna'. Here was I, enveloped in a huge feather bed, with a little girl at one side of me and a baby boy in the crook of one arm. He was well wrapped up against the winterish weather."

Capna', the highest farm on Malham Moor, stood with its back to Knowle Fell, which adjoins Fountains Fell, at 2,170 ft. A clump of sycamore at the back of the buildings offered some bield [shelter]. The farm was fed from a spring on Black Hill – a source of water that had never been known to dry up, even in the most parched summer. Indeed, several springs surfaced on this large patch of boggy land where no less than five parishes met.

One flow of water met Gorbecks and passed Cowside Farm, coursing round the hill to the twin-falls of Catterick Foss and Stainforth, where in addition to a bridge the beck had a set of ancient stepping stones. This flow of water joined Old Man Ribble. Other springs emanating on Black Hill seeped into Streets Pasture, emerging at water holes below the grey face of Malham Cove, a bow-shaped limestone cliff that provided the dale with its spectacular headpiece.

Charles Kingsley, a visitor to Malham Tarn House, an imaginative writer, populated the beck with water-babies.

A Farm with a View

EDITH WOULD never forget her first view of Capna' when they journeyed to take it over. They went via Helwith Bridge and Langcliffe. When they got to the top of the steep brow, the land was not green, as it had been at Austwick. There was a scattering of snow. Penyghent, rising from limestone pavements, was as white as a shroud. They travelled on. The snow deepened. "When we got to the top of the hill, we could see Malham Tarn in the distance. Near at hand, to the left, was Capna'. I thought: 'What a wilderness. How am I going to settle here'?"

Robert led the horse and its heaped-up load along the lane to Capna'. "The first house you come to is a cottage-style house, and round the corner is the farmhouse, We went into the yard. There was snow on the ground. All the dubs were covered with shot-ice. Granny Carr was waiting for us. She had made a big fire in the living room." They sat by the fire until they were warmed through. The child was fed. Granny went home. "We sorted out our furniture and, while Robert went round the sheep, I prepared the beds. Then, late at night, we talked. We had great hopes for our stay at this remote place."

Edith's first impression as she entered Capna' had been one of horror. "Mrs Robinson had been an ill woman for a long time and had not been able to do much. The place was draughty. The ceilings were covered with what looked suspiciously like brown paper. Gaps under the doors were so big you could nearly walk through them. I thought to myself: 'What am I going to do with this big house to get it liveable'?"

There were four rooms on the ground floor and four large bedrooms. Taking up an entire wall in the older part of the farmhouse was a sandstone inglenook, seven feet high and six feet deep. At each side lay beehive-type ovens, of the type in which bread was once made, though the stones of one of them were bleached white, giving Edith the feeling that it had been used for the storage of salt, which must be kept dry. Salt was needed in preserving pigmeat and mutton for winter use.

In the old days, cooking would take place over an open fire which, Edith presumed, was made of peat and coal sledded down from Fountains Fell. "I had my suspicions that at the far end of the sitting room there was something under the flagged floor. This spot was cracked and uneven. Later, during alterations, were found traces of what had been a central fireplace. Capna' was most certainly old."

As time went on, Edith grew to love the old house. "The house seemed to mellow into me." She could even tolerate its ghosts. Late at night she heard doors being opened and closed several times. She saw a human form lying on an iron-framed bed kept in the back bedroom. "I am not a nervous person, but I fled and did not return to that room for several days. When I plucked up courage to enter, all was peaceful. On the morning I thought I had seen a ghost, Granny Shackleton, who had brought me up, passed away."

Two years went by before Edith got the proverbial "straight edge" and was able to devote a little more time to researching into the history of Capna'. There had been half a dozen variants of the name since the 12th century. Fountains Abbey acquired most of Malham Moor, to the foot of Penyghent. Thomas Benson and Robert Peococke were tenants at "Capna," paying an annual rent of 53s.2d.

In the 16th century, John and Henry Peococke, sons of Robert, had an agreement regarding the farm and rights on "ffountamus ffell." In 1600, Thomas Peocoke passed on his tenancy of "Cappn-ferme," the document being witness and signed by George, one of the illustrious Cliffords, being Lord of the Manor. Thomas Carr, of Hunsthwaite, Settle, was the next tenant, followed by his widow Jennett.

In 1629, the tenancy passed to Stephen Fish, a wealthy family who lived at Winterburn Hall and also owned land at Stockdale and Rough Close. These, and Capon Hall, were referred to as The Estate. Stephen married Martha Ferrand, the youngest daughter of Benjamin Ferrand of Harden, near Bingley. She was herself wealthy, bringing a dowry of £2,000, to be paid over a period of two years.

Moorland Sensations

EDITH HAD first visited Malham Moor while living at Hanlith. It was not a moor in the Bronte sense of peat and heather, though this occurred at higher levels on Fountains and Darnbook Fells. Much of the parish of Malham Moor was on limestone. The fields held short, sweet grass and an abundance of flowers with pastel shades.

Edith has written of her first experience of this high ground: "The plaintive cries of the birds pierced the stillness. I heard the strange burring noise of a snipe. A grey-faced ewe bleated a warning to her lambs, which sheltered from the prevailing wind behind tufts of cotton grass. Towering mountains formed a backcloth, their dappled summits being almost perpetually enveloped in cloud." Malham Tarn was "mirroring the chasing clouds, a thousand bobbing waves created by the wind bearing down from Fountains Fell."

Among "all this loneliness," and close to Black Hill, was the farm that was to be her home for a large part of her married life. The panoramic view from Capna' land took in the Grisedale fells, Thoragill Fell and Darnbrook Fell, with Great Whernside towering behind. To the fore were Pikedaw and Kirkby Fell. The fells of Cracoe and Rylstone, together with Rombald's Moor merged with the Lancashire moors and Pendle Hill.

Capna' had once presided over a considerable estate. Since then, the centre of attention had moved to Malham Tarn House, which had belonged to millionaire Walter Morrison up to his death in 1922 and was now owned by kinsfolk. Morrison, who was treated with all the respect due to a wealthy man, had a big house in London. He visited Tarn House mainly in the summer.

Elsewhere, some of the scattering of farms had evolved from the huts of shepherds who had cared for flocks of sheep belonging to Fountains Abbey. The shepherds drove the sheep to the grange at Kilnsey, in

Wharfedale, when the time came for them to be washed, then clipped. The valuable fleeces were transported over the Grassington moors to the Abbey in ox-hauled wains.

Edith was enthralled by tales told of Abraham Banks, one of the last generation to live when farms were virtually inaccessible in winter and those who lived there needed strength of character and constitution. In Abraham's boyhood, in the 19th century, oatmeal porridge was his main diet. White bread and tea were regarded as a Sunday treat. His mother made oatcake on a backstone. She produced home-brewed beer, also hard cheese, made from skimmed milk. Each year, a stirk or bullock was killed and hung for winter use. The oil lamp was reserved for the reading of the *Craven Herald*. Otherwise, light came from home-made candles. His mother and sisters made his clothes until he was a man, when his clothing needs and those of the other men in the family were met by a travelling tailor.

Edith soon recognised that the weather dominated life on Malham Moor. In spring, the limestone was bone-white against the blue-black of a passing thundercloud. On a rare calm day in summer, a light haze might hang over the moor, softening the outlines of the fells and walls. On a black-and-silver day in October, even the wet limestone assumed a dark appearance, while the black clouds had silver linings. A low-slung sun would illuminate the dripping walls and plate them with silver.

When I visited the moorland farms in the 1950s, it was a day that, according to one farmer, "looks as though it's bin up aw neet." Another said: "We're having some rum showers. It's clashy bad weather for the stock. We're near the clouds and get all the winds that blow. There's not a reight lot o' bield [shelter] up here." His farm man had braved the elements and departed for Skipton with some sheep. Said the farmer, with dry Dales humour and the merest flicker of a smile: "He likes to think he's t'boss. I don't mind – as long as he does t'work!"

Measurable amounts of rain occur on an average of over 200 days. There might be snow cover for 220 days. The mist can be thick and damp, like a wet dish-clout. At Darnbrook, one of the big old sheep

24

Continued on page 33

Above: A Victorian study of Hanlith Hall Farm, which was to become Edith's home for many years. *Below:* The Shackleton family – Grandmother Paulina, nursing Pattie; Alice (Edith's mother), Jonas and Grandfather Tom. (Alice and Jonas died during the same week in the 1918 influenze epidemic).

Rookery Farm, Winterburn, where the Shackletons farmed for twelve years. In the picture below, Tom and Ernest are clipping sheep.

Above: Mastiles Lane, crossing the broad acres to the east of Malham Moor.
Below: A Swaledale tup, the hardy Pennine breed of sheep.

Scenes from an Arctic Winter

Left: A team of men with shovels attempt to clear Henside Lane, between Cowside and Capna'. Wind and further snow nullified their efforts.
Below, left: Lee Gate, where Robert Carr lived until his marriage to Edith.
Below: Snow-cutters and the postman – the unsung heroes of the Big Snow of February, 1947.

Right: Edith Shackleton, aged 20, riding Cherry at Hanlith Hall Farm, Malhamdale. In 1939, she joined the Women's Land Army but continued to work at her grandparents' farm.

Left: A dreary March 1st, 1943, is enlivened by the wedding at Kirkby Malham of Edith and Robert Carr. They spent their honeymoon at the home of friends in Blackpool.

Above: Malham Tarn House, the former "mountain home" of Walter Morrison, and later to become a field centre, introducing many to the natural splendours of the district. *Below:* Friars Head, Winterburn, where Jim and Minnie Taylor had a welcome for Edith, who called on her walk home from school.

Above: Caponhow, adjacent to Capon Hall. The names of this moorland farm have changed with a bewildering regularity. *Below:* Sheep farming on Malham Moor could not take place without the collie, a quick means of rounding up the flock.

farms, on that autumn day of long ago, George Robinson told me: "Winter can make a start as now and carry on till nearly May. There's late growth up here. We don't often see an improvement till June." As another vicious hail shower began to develop, we scurried into the doorway of an outbuilding. The fury of the wind competed with the growl of Darnbrook beck in flood conditions.

The beck surged under a bridge that was the successor of one dating back to 1541 when Ralph Buke of Darnbrook willed "6s.8d to the making of the bridge afore my doore if my nebors will make it." A gate spans the road at the modern bridge. Once there were half a dozen and more gates to be opened (and closed again) on the road from Langcliffe to Arncliffe. Old Dr Hyslop of Settle got special payment, when attending a patient, because he (or someone he took with him) had to open and close gates no less than sixteen times.

Darnbrook has more land over than under 1,200 ft and and no less than 25 miles of drystone walls. In 1942 the farm was snowed up for ten weeks. Five years later, half of the flock was lost. The animals "hungered to death." Malham Moor is mainly sheep country. Over 80 per cent of the livestock consists of self-contained breeding flocks of tough sheep descended from the indigenous stock.

Near-neighbours of Edith and Robert, Mason Hodgson and his wife, lived at Tennant Gill. Mr Mason was progressive in his farming methods. He had a special type of cattle, a cross between Friesian/Aberdeen Angus and a Hereford bull. The beasts were in-wintered and fattened up during the following summer, using land in the Settle District. He fattened his wether and shot gimmer lambs in the meadows, so that by the time they were sold they were worth double the normal price. The sheep had extra rations – clover hay and hard, round blocks of nourishing foods.

When foxes were courting, in winter, Edith would hear the mewing of the vixen and the yapping of the dog fox. It was not uncommon, at the edge o'dark, to see foxes crossing the meadows on their way from Black Hill on to the high fell. One March, a commuting fox could not resist snapping off the heads of twin lambs. Black Hill was a strange tract of land, with craters left where bombs had been exploded and soft spots where the unwary would find themselves up to their waists in the cloying peat. On an especially noisy day, a squad of kilted Scotsmen playing bagpipes passed the farm, coming from who-knows? They were heading for who-knows-where?

Edith says, wistfully: "Some people can't make a home. It's a house, isn't it? If you've anything about you, you make a home, wherever it is." She always felt elated when, on a rare trip from the farm, she came back within sight of Capna', the Tarn and the Scars, and she wrote:

> *At the summit of the hill*
> *Just pause a moment there –*
> *The Moor before and the Dale behind*
> *Was any place more fair?*

Nowt but Work

IN THE late 1940s, life was Spartan. "I was weary and, at night, glad to get the little ones to bed. Then I could try and catch up with my baking or washing. The keen air gave us all good appetites. Bread, pies and cakes were needed. Rock buns were in endless demand."

At the end of May or in early June, weather permitting, the sheep were shorn. The sheep must be gathered dry-backed. "We fell asleep to the bleating of ewes and lambs that had to be penned up so as to be handy for shearing. After a sleepless night, we rose, dressed in our oldest clothes and set to with a will." It was in the days of when neighbours were close friends, ever-willing to help. Folk from nearby farms arrived to give Edith and Robert a hand.

They, mindful that crisp air and hard work would sharpen the appetites of their helpers, killed a sheep, which meant that there was a copious stock of mutton. Pies and jam pasties were baked. Edith recalls taking down from a hook on the ceiling a large ham that had been maturing for over a year. "I stood it in a bowl of cold water overnight to soak. So much of the salt was drawn out before the ham was cooked."

The baking bowl was brought out and a lump of dough made and rolled on a floured board until it was about an inch thick, whereupon the ham was set on it and the dough drawn over to enclose it. The fat and the salt seeped into the dough as it cooked. After about four hours cooking in the big oven, the crust was taken off, the rind scored and put back to turn a lovely golden brown. The ham made its appearance in sandwiches.

The earthen floor of the back-barn was brushed clean and two large wooden doors were laid on the floor. Wooden stocks [stools, long enough to accommodate sheep and clipper] were brought out. Huge sacks were suspended on cotton ropes from beams over the barn porch and were ready to receive the fleeces. Tar and markers were at hand. So were tins of red and blue ruddle. "All was ready except the shears. They were lifted down from their shelf, where they had been kept preserved in oiled rags since the last clipping."

When clipping began, clogs were heard clacking and skidding over greasy cobbles. Ewes struggled briefly as they were handed to the shearers, and placed on the wooden benches. "The ewes were uneasy. Sweat poured from the men as they clipped their way round the sheep's neck, then down the belly, peeling off the flanks, clipping down the back and finishing at the tail end. There was fierce competition between the men. A good average for clipping was twenty sheep an hour."

The fleeces were laid on the doors, prior to being rolled, sheared side downwards, turning in the flanks and rolling from the tail end. A coil of wool was pulled from the neck-end and twisted so that the oily bundle might be tied.

Near where the clippers were at work stood a large can of tea that was continually being emptied and re-filled. It slaked many a parched throat. "Before a sheep was released, the lips were parted and the shearer glanced at the teeth, judging the age of the animal. Draft ewes, which would be disposed off in the autumn, were marked with a red blob on their topping. The farm marks were added to the area of the ribs, using tar, and ruddle was smeared on the huggins. And off a shorn sheep would go with a plaintive bleat to rejoin the flock."

Meanwhile, in the house, the meal was being prepared. Soap and towels were laid by the sink. At a signal, the men trooped into the house, quickly washed, then crowded around the old oak table, laughing and chiding each other as they ate their fill. Pints of ale were passed round. In the evening, when the last ewe had been clipped, the sheep were returned to their pastures at Black Hill and Gorbecks, being directed there by the faithful old dogs, Laddie and Jess. With them was a pup, learning the points of sheep-driving.

At Austwick, the grass had been thick and lush. Here, on Malham Moor, it was laggard. Then, with the summer sun upon it, the fields came on with a rush. Robert visited Skipton to hire an Irishman to help with the hay harvest. Old Abraham had told of the day he rode a young horse to hire an Irish haymaker in Skipton. The Irishman had a tin trunk. It was borne triumphantly home on the back of the young horse.

In the days of Edith and Robert, the Men of Erin stood outside the Hole in the Wall inn. The Irishman selected by Robert was, unlike many of his compatriots, an idle sort of fellow. He preferred drinking or feasting to work. "We sent him packing and got a better man. At last we managed to get the hay into the barns." The Irish labourers were, to quote Robert, a "right comical lot," except that at haytime nothing that happened was truly funny.

Robert set off an Irishman named Patrick with a swathe-turner. He must cover a big flat field and finish the work without any trouble. Robert, having told him to start in the next field, moved away. There were two gates, one wide, one narrow, leading into that "next field" and Patrick chose to take the horse and swathe-turner through the narrow one, which was intended for the use of animals. "When we looked out of the farmhouse window, there was the sorry sight of a bewildered Patrick. He had tried to drive through the narrow gateway. The horse, having pulled the shafts off the machine, had kept walking, with the shafts in train. There was Pat, perched on the seat of the machine, with the wheels and the rear-end of the machine around him. He explained: 'The machine was too wide and the walls came up to meet me'."

Another day, Pat was sent to the bottom meadow – a grand flat field – where he was put on the tractor, an old Fordson. It had only one speed – slow. The grass-mower was yoked on behind. He was so intent on driving straight round the field, he never noticed the pin attaching the mower to the tractor had fallen out. To his amazement, the next time round, he met with the stationary mower. Robert, cursing, signalled him to stop. Pat went on, with sweat dripping off his nose end, looking neither right or left. "We were always glad to see Patrick arrive. We were also thankful when he returned to Ireland. There were always calamities when he was around."

On Sundays, the Irishmen met up at the Listers at Malham for a day of boozing, which meant that on the following day they were not in the mood for work. "Robert would be trying to spur our Irishmen on, uttering strong threats. Sometimes, they would put on a spurt for half an hour. Then they'd sneak off to sit at the wallside, holding their heads or even falling asleep. Robert would let out a big roar. The labourers would nearly jump out of their skins and start off again."

After haytime, they looked forward to the lamb sales, a primary source of income. There was enough money to take the children off to Morecambe for the day; they talked about it for weeks afterwards.

There had been a most trying day, just after the war, when the cows broke out of their field and set off down the road. Robert quickly mounted the pony, which was named Tony, and galloped after them. Edith and the children, looking out of the farmhouse, were concerned when they saw the cows wandering about the road with the horse standing nearby. Where was Robert? Karl, the German who was helping the family, was sent to investigate and he returned saying: "Boss has broken his back or a leg." It was with difficulty that Robert, a 17-stone man, was lifted into the horse and cart they took to collect him.

Robert was, of course, in acute pain and his language was not of the best. Getting him on to the cart was a slow and painstaking job. At least, he had not broken his back. His leg was undoubtedly fractured. Back in the yard of Capna', there was a debate as to what to do with him. Karl was sent to Lee Gate to summon Robert's brother, Frank. "He had just got a Ford 8 car. It was very small. Like a box on wheels." Robert was driven to Skipton hospital, which like others was having to cope with the introduction of the National Health Service. A chit from the injured person's doctor was needed. Robert was driven back and when a note was provided by Dr Lovett he was returned to the hospital.

Still they would not deal with him. "There was Robert, full of asprins, cursing away or moaning that 'I've had it'. We managed to get him home and into a bed we set up near the living room window. Frank went off home. Granny had an idea that it would be best to pay for treatment, and this we did. A Skipton doctor set his leg. There was no anaesthetic. The pain knocked poor Robert out. For three days he was off his rocker. Then he began to perk up. Came the time he said he would be able to drive again. He had a stick to press the clutch down."

Forty-Seven Winter

THE HAY crop of 1946 was poor. Would the weather remain mild so that the cattle might be kept outdoors until late autumn? The Weather Clerk was in a peevish mood. Winter came early, with hard frost overnight and with snowflakes dancing in the wind during the day. There was the usual mild spell just before Christmas. In the New Year, the dalesfolk entered the main snow season.

On Sunday, February 2, 1947, the grimmest winter in the memory of the Dalesfolk began with a snowstorm. Mercifully, no one had knowledge of the hard conditions that lay ahead or they would have capitulated. Not until the end of March would the snow-cutters clear the last of the big drifts and the cores of old drifts would remain in shady places until June.

A north-easterly brought snow that stuck and eventually even squeaked. Snow blown off the fields and fells blocked the roads, creating drifts up to 15 ft high. They changed the usual contours of the land. Sheep were overblown. Brown hares had their normal food supply cut off. The farmfolk were isolated.

Gangs of men who laboriously cleared a stretch of road one day found it had infilled when they returned the following morning. At Nether Hesleden, in nearby Littondale, the farmer and his helpers excavated a tunnel through snow for over twenty yards in order to reach the big barn.

Towards dusk, on February 21, 1947, Edith, her family and Karl, the German prisoner of war who was lodging with them, became aware of the true nature of this terrible winter. Having experienced a bitterly cold day, in which every room was a meeting place for cutting drafts, the Carr family huddled over the old range in the kitchen. "We were wearing layers of woollies and toasting our chilblains" is how Edith described the situation. To go outdoors was to enter a polar wilderness.

The children gazed on the world through peep-holes they made on the rime obscuring the windows. "We could see ice-bound tracks in snow. We also saw a few miserable sheep, almost completely covered with snow. Not being able to dig down to the grass because of frost-crusted snow, they were bleating pitifully for hay."

The sun gave off hardly any warmth during the day. Just before it set behind Black Hill, the frosty world was tinted red. Then it would begin to snow again. The clouds that deposited the crisp flakes resembled smoke billowing from a subterranean boiler. "It went on week after week – this hard frost, this red light, this searching north-east wind and yet more snow."

Eventually, you might cross the landscape walking over the walls.

Frost put a thick crust of ice on the becks and tarns. "A lot of farmers on Malham Moor, and especially those at High Trenhouse, fetched water in milk kits from a spring on Black Hill. Fortunately, that spring didn't dry up. They needed the water for the cows as well as the kitchens. It's surprising how much water a cow can drink. As for the people, there wasn't much washing went on!"

That wintry spell of February and March, 1947, almost ruined the farmers. Edith and her family survived for a time on brown hares, cooked in various ways. The hares came down from the fells in large numbers and foraged for food around the farm.

As the days went by, the household began to run out of food. It was tantalising to think of the old days at Granny's home in Winterburn, when food was plentiful. Mr Hardisty, the butcher, would arrive on Thursdays by horse and trap. The Friday meal was a favourite of Edith – mostly liver and dumplings, which Granny had made out of yeast dough. It was tantalising to recall the setting and the meal.

Granny would pick up her oven cloth, open the iron door of the black-leaded range and set a huge brown stewpot on the table. She would lift the lid, revealing the dumplings, now bubbling in the stew, all golden and brown, and fill up Edith's plate with the delicious food. Granny would then take mashed potatoes out of an iron pot simmering on the top rib of the fire grate. The two combined as the main course in a memorable meal.

Like every other old farm on the Moor, Capna' had a stone-flagged kitchen and pantry. And as at Granny's house, the dominant feature of the kitchen was a big iron range, incorporating a fireplace, side-oven and boiler. On baking day, it was vital to get every trace of soot out of the flues. "You had to get your hand right up the chimney to clean out at the top of the oven with a cowl-rake. Then you got a goose-wing and dusted inside the oven. There was another flue at the side. You must get all these clean before you started baking.

"The next job was to fill the boiler and have a bucket of coal and wood ready for stoking up. When the fire was 'drawing' well, the latch on the oven door was closed to get your heat. You opened the latch when baking bread to let the steam out. Otherwise the bread would be soggy. Done properly, and it was lovely and crusty." Pots, pans and the ingredients for baking were brought out of the pantry, which contained benks [shelves] made of flagstone brought from quarries at Helwith Bridge.

That was in the past. The present situation was increasingly desperate. As the food stock at Capna' dwindled, so did the cattle fodder in the barn. "The cows were 'bawling' all day. We could not feed them too much at a time and they were permanently hungry. Then there would be more frost or snow. All was engulfed."

When the storm eased, Robert donned his greatcoat and, with the extra warmth provided by scarf and cap, set off on horseback to get some food. He returned at dusk with a little food, some potatoes and porridge oats, which were hanging from the horse's back. Then their German helper was persuaded to take the horse down to Settle for food. He was away for such a long time that Robert was alarmed. When the horse returned without its rider, Robert went looking for the missing man and found him blundering about. He was assisted back to the warm kitchen. "Next day," recalls Edith, "we could trace his wavering journey back to the farm by the bits and pieces of groceries he had dropped on the snow."

The postmen took turns, day after day, to walk the four miles from

Langcliffe to the farmsteads on Malham Moor. The mail was frequently left at Capna' to await collection by neighbouring farmers. When a postman entered the kitchen in the early afternoon, he was a sorry sight, his outer clothes stiff with the cold and his eyebrows and hair covered with rime.

Mr Chaffers, short and stout, was determined that the snow would not stop His Majesty's mail from getting through. He arrived at Capna' with great ceremony, puffing and blowing. He would then unpeel his waterproof leggings and the brown paper and newspaper he had wrapped round his legs, securing the wrapping with thick, coarse string. He had great faith in this 'thermal' wear.

Edith never ceased to be amazed at the way he trundled for miles when he was like a well-wrapped parcel. When the round became too much for him, it was allocated to three other postmen who visited the Moor on alternate days. Mr Verden, a lively chap, was looking pleased with himself when he entered the kitchen one day. He joked about the weather, then said: "Get the frying pan on! They'll be here in no time." He was referring to a team of snow-cutters and a bulldozer from Thornton and Garnett's at Rathmell who had reached Cowside Farm and were just over two miles away from Capna'. They had to face the "drag" up Henside Lane, which the drifting snow had filled level with the wall-tops. They must also negotiate the bottom side of Dick Close Pasture and High Fell.

A day or two later, the drone of the bulldozer working its way to the farm might be heard at Capna'. It was the only sound to break the stillness of Malham Moor. The cavalcade arrived. Each man carried a wax candle while snow cutting and continually rubbed it against his shovel so that the snow would glide off as they threw it to one side.

At last they reached the lane end to Capna'. Here a huge snowdrift that had given much delight to the children confronted them. This had always been a windy corner, especially in winter when – as Edith said – the wind "whipped the snow like a huge ice-cream cone." Now, with relief at hand, all worked with a will to dig a passage through the great drift. "Good, we thought; now we are almost free."

Tragedy struck when Mr Bullock, one of the Council workmen, slipped from the side of the high drift into the path of the oncoming snowplough. His mates were stunned and shocked. As they stood there, wondering what to do, another snowstorm began and the day's work was being undone as the road filled in again. Mr Bullock was wrapped in a top coat and carried to Capna'. Edith and her family were unaware of the drama until there was a loud knock at the door. She thought the men would be seeking hot water for a "brew." Edith was amazed to see a pathetic, huddled group of men carrying the limp form of their former colleague. Mr Bullock was laid before the fire, but he was already beyond human help.

Edith attended to the shocked workmen, boiling some water and filling the pan with eggs taken from a waterglass, an old-fashioned form of egg preservative. Each man had some toast, a boiled egg and a pot of tea. For several days, there was no more snow-digging. Happily, the thaw was at hand. And there was high drama when the RAF dropped bales of hay for the starving stock. No one ordered the hay. To this day, Edith has no idea where it came from or who paid for it. As far as she and Robert were concerned, it was manna from heaven.

News of the air-drop of supplies was first given when an old postman arrived at the farm day and said: "They've gotten word through that you're just about on your beam-ends." He had heard on the radio that the RAF were organising a mercy-flight from Dishforth to the remote farms with food and fodder. Edith asked him when they would be coming. He said: "All being well, it should be tomorrow."

The postman had also heard on the radio that those affected should, if possible, make a big cross on the snow. So, in the morning, Edith and Robert made a large cross of "provin" sacks and old motor oil. It stood out clearly against the frozen snow. "We waited and listened, ready to put a match to the oil. At about half past two, we went out and we started this big fire. It threw out a lot of smoke. True enough, about three o' clock, we could hear droning aeroplanes coming. I thought – great! We got in the house to be out of the way of anything that was dropped. When I went in, our children were underneath the living room table.

They had been scared by the sound of the planes.

"The planes flew round the house once or twice, just to make sure it was 'it', and got so low we could see the doors opening. First of all, they dropped us big parcels of food. Robert ran across and picked them up. Then they went away and came back in a short while, flying over the front meadow, dropping bales of hay. Unfortunately, as the bales hit the ground, they burst open. We could hardly turn the animals out to eat it in the field because there was deep snow. I thought they'd be breaking their legs or something.

"We tussled and we tussled for the rest of the day and just about all night getting most of the hay under cover. There was quite a bit of hay left, so Robert brought the sheep that had been in the croft at the side of the house into the front meadow. They had the time of their lives running from one clump of hay to another. It was a matter of which sheep got to the hay quickest. So we were rescued..."

The Carr family remained in good health during the trying times. The raw winds that tried to cut through to the bone also put a ruddy complexion on everyone's faces. When Edith was alone in the house – the rest of the family had gone off with sheepdogs and clothes props, intent on finding sheep that had been overblown by snow – an accident occurred. She was taking the coal scuttle across the yard for another supply of fuel when she slipped on ice and fell heavily. Shaken and in pain, she staggered back to the kitchen and crept on to the nearest chair.

"I felt sick. My left arm ached. My wrist was mis-shapen." When the children returned, they gathered round. It would soon be dusk and Robert would not have time to surmount the snowdrift and contact the doctor in Settle. Edith's grandfather used to tell of a quarryman who had his leg badly crushed. The shafts of shovels were used as splints. "I looked round the kitchen and then set to work using butter-pats and bandages as splints. I tied them using my good hand and my teeth. To be a survivor on Malham Moor, you have to make-do and improvise. That's what gives the dalesfolk their independent spirit."

The Great Snow ended. The Malham Moorers counted the cost. At Capna', the family had almost run out of provisions. Twenty-two head of cattle and about 120 lambing sheep had died. The milk flow of the surviving cattle fell off so much that the animals went dry. Sheep that had been so weak they could hardly stand around contrived, in the spring, to produce a larger-than-average crop of lambs. "It was a disaster. Everywhere you looked, there were dead lambs and dead sheep."

There was a day when Robert, standing in the yard, called out for Edith to join him. They stood in the silence. Then their faces lit up. Across the moor came the bubbling call of a curlew. By April, conditions had moderated. The Carr children went back to school after being snowbound for nine weeks.

A Changing World

EDITH HAD the care of four children. After the war, the folk living on the Moor were investing in motor vehicles, and though petrol was still rationed there was a lively demand among dalesfolk for ex-Army jeeps – robust vehicles suited to progress both on and off the road.

"The first thing we had that went on four wheels with an engine was something very special. One day, I heard a roaring sound in the yard and went out to see something like a big tank. I thought: 'What the heck has Robert got now?' It was an Army vehicle – so big it was an effort to climb up into the cab. Robert said: 'This will just be right if it comes snowy'."

"I kept thinking about how much petrol it would need. Robert said he hadn't thought of that. He didn't keep it for long because I was nattering at him all the time. I said: 'I'm not going to ride in that'. Then we got a jeep. Everyone on the Moor seemed to get a jeep. There were jeeps whizzing about in all directions."

The family had stopped milking cows by this time, mainly because in the bad winters the milk wagon could not reach the farm. Rather than pour away the milk, Edith was inclined to make some butter, as she had done years before when living with her Granny. There had been a time when the tenant of Capna' had made cheese. "There was along the back passage of Capna' a long dark room, lined with narrow slate shelves. I'm pretty sure it was a room where cheese were put and turned regularly till they ripened."

Butter-making involved separating cream from the milk, which Edith did using "leads,"which were shallow trays with sloping sides. When a plug was removed after a while, the "blue" milk flowed away and the cream was left on the sides. The thick cream was skimmed off into a pot using a metal skimmer.

A special day was set aside for churning. The cream pot was placed in front of a hot fire and was turned at intervals until the cream was at blood-heat. "You'd be churning forever if you didn't get it to the right temperature. When my cream was warming up, I got my churn ready. We had an end-over-end churn. It was a big wooden thing on a frame. I poured in two gallons of boiling water, turned the churn a few times, then let it stand it for about five minutes. It was warming the wood and also sterilising it. This ensured that the butter would not stick.

"I let the water out and immediately poured in cream from the pot, clamping down the top of the churn. The actual churning could now begin. If I was lucky it would 'turn' in about a quarter of an hour or twenty minutes. I could sense it bumping when the butter curds were coming together. There was a little glass at the top of the churn. If it came clean, that was the time to draw a drop of the butter milk out and put some cold water in, about two quarts.

"The butter needed to be 'washed' three times with clean water before being drawn off. When I screwed off the top, and the gas came out, there was this lovely smell. I'd tip the butter into a wooden butter bowl that had been scalded out. I had some big slates, which were also scalded. On to them went the butter-pats to be 'worked' using a rolling pin, backwards and forwards, until every drop of water was removed. Otherwise the butter would be too strong and would not keep."

The processed butter was weighed into round pounds for domestic use. An alternative was to sell it or barter with a retailer on the next visit to town.

Modern Times

THE BIG SNOWS of 1947 and 1963 were the last great natural trials for the Dales farmers. "After that, the weather's got milder. It's a different climate. It's like spring nearly all the time compared with what it was then." No one minded a smattering of snow at Christmas, though one year events on Christmas Day itself took an unexpected turn. Edith had volunteered to help Robert with the milking so that it would be over early, allowing the family to have the traditional "lovely time."

A conifer was felled to provide them with a tree that they promptly decorated, not with fairy lights – as today – but with small candles set in little holders that clipped on to the branches. Edith's last words to her children as she left to help with the milking were: "Don't touch the Christmas tree. On no account light the candles till I come." Edith went outside. The milking took place. "We always used a lot of milk and so I went into the house and left two big jugs of milk on the kitchen table. And I went back to the shippon.

Seconds later, or so it seemed, Anne appeared shouting: "Mother! Mother! The Christmas tree's on fire!" Edith had a sudden vision of the house being burnt down on Christmas Day. "I flew into the house. You never, in your life, saw anything like it. Apparently, as soon as I got out of the way, someone had put a match to one of the candles. Having a flickering flame, it kindled the cotton wool and the dry branches. The Christmas tree went up in flames.

"Our Anne did have the presence of mind to go into the kitchen. The first things she clapped her eyes on were these two jugs of milk. She slashed the milk on to the Christmas tree. Luckily, it doused the flames. But the mess was indescribable. The cotton wool was blackened and hung in tatters, dripping with milk. On the carpet under the tree was a big pool of milk. The smell of burnt milk was awful. As you might imagine, there was a troubled household that Christmas Day. The day after was the worst for me. I had to get all the carpet up. What was left of the Christmas tree had to go out. It was shocking."

It had been Calamity Year. Most times, when accidents occurred, Edith was on her own, with no telephone for summoning help. Robert was either with his friends or had gone to market. Stephen had a tricycle which ran away with him. He grazed himself so badly on the garden wall that Dr Leo O'Connor of Settle used twelve stitches to repair the worst of the damage.

Then it was young Robin's turn to injure himself. Mounting the pony, he rode him around at the best possible speed, re-living scenes from films that featured the cowboy Roy Rogers. The pony arrived back at the farm without its spirited rider and Robin was found lying on the ground, his face and teeth re-shaped. Hurriedly he was taken to the surgery of the O'Connors at Settle, where the assistance of a dentist was needed. Robin was stitched up. Happily, he did not suffer any permanent injury nor lasting scars.

Years later, he came to grief when his Lambretta scooter skidded on a cow-pat as he returned home. Capna' was still without a telephone. Edith had to rush to a farmhouse, a mile away, to ring the doctor. An ambulance was sent. Robin was taken to Leeds Infirmary at dead of night. Edith stayed with him for two days – and then made a daily journey to visit him until he was out of danger.

The appearance of the Moor changed with "improvements" to farming. The hill farmers were given a subsidy, part of which was to be spent on artificial fertilisers to be spread on the land. "They thought they were improving the meadows. They were getting more grass but destroying the lovely herby stuff that produced what we used to call 'sheep hay'." What had been "flower fields," with a host of diminutive flowers, took on a tedious shade of green from ryegrass that was better able to sustain a rising population of cattle.

When the National Trust acquired the Tarn Estate, part of the estate, including the big house, was leased to the Field Studies Council. Paul Holmes, his wife Mary and their daughters moved in. With the arrival of parties of students and, to quote Edith, "motors running up and down," the Moor sprang to unaccustomed life. "When I saw a big orange bus passing on its way to Tarn House, we could scarcely believe our eyes and I thought: "'This is the start of things to come'. And it was!"

Malham Moor had its own school, situated near the Tarn. "My husband's sister, Doris Carr – Auntie Doris to our kids – was the last teacher. She used to commute from Lee Gate on a pony. When the school was closed, our children were collected by taxi and taken to Settle. It was a bit of a headache. When it came wild in winter, and your children were away at Settle, you were left wondering if they would ever get home."

One day, life on Malham Moor took a horrific turn when a low-flying aircraft burst into flames and crashed, killing all those within it. Jim Jackson, who swept the limestone roads, clipped the grass verges and kept the drains clear on a three mile long stretch, representing the old way of life. "The roads were a credit to him. We enjoyed his company when he called at the farm for a brew-up."

In an area where life could have been hum-drum, some of the farmers enlivened it with their drinking and their antics. Much of the drinking was done at the hostelries of Malham. The wartime antics included turning the road signs so that they faced in the opposite direction, confusing any potential enemy and also any strangers who were on lawful business.

Trout, on their spawning run in the becks flowing into Malham Tarn, were poached, having been attracted to the poacher by powerful lights. When four-wheel drive vehicles came into use, there were nocturnal quests for brown hares, the driver using his knowledge of local topography to keep the vehicle out of trouble and t'main chap, complete with powerful light, sitting on the bonnet. The light disorientated the hares.

Some of the farmers regarded Capna' as a social centre and called now and again, demolishing a couple of apple pies before settling down to a game of dominoes, followed by a few rounds of arm-wrestling. Another time, the visitors would join Robert in a game or two of cards, staying occasionally until it early next morning, when it was almost milking time.

Edith baked almost every day for the family and for visitors. One caller at Capna' was impressed by Robert's appetite when he saw him with a leg of lamb in one hand and a knife in the other. The knife was being used to pare the meat. He was eating his way down to the bone.

A good supply of beer was maintained by Edith at haytime. She made "botanical beer" in two large baking bowls, using purchased ingredients to which were added 4 lb of sugar and 2 lb of raisins. A piece of toast covered with yeast was floated on the concoction. When the toast became soggy, the yeast was able to do its work. This type of beer was drunk in considerable quantities.

Until a tractor was bought for Capna', "haytime was a right tussle, I can tell you. A lot of the land was steep and we tried to get as much as we could. We had a single-horse mowing machine first. One single horse – going round and round the fields. Then we got a double-horse machine. When the horse machine had got it cut, it was all to rake and turn by hand."

When electricity came to Malham Moor, the domestic revolution was complete. Each farmer promised to pay a tariff at the time of installation. The Capna' payment was £100, which was by no means petty cash at that time. "Gone at last were the dim candle lights in our bedrooms. Gone were the smelly paraffin lamps on the table downstairs. And gone was the hissing 'hurricane lamp,' hanging from a hook on the wall of an outbuilding.

A falling lamp struck Robert's head the day before the switch-on, and he was knocked out. Robert, having quickly recovered, resumed his daily routine and took advantage of the coming of electricity, arriving home with a washing machine he had bought from Mr Sutcliffe, a milkman at Foulridge, for £5. The machine was "an antiquated thing – like a big green tub standing on a frame. It had like a paddle in the middle that worked backwards and forwards. It hadn't a lid or anything. There was just this paddle, going backwards and forwards, backwards and forwards. It made such a big noise."

Edith waited, thrilled and spellbound, as the plug was put into the socket. "Yes, it really worked. It hadn't a wringer attached to it, so I had to use my old ringing machine – the one with the wooden rollers. But there would be no more hours spent at the dolly tub and the rubbing board. I washed everything I could lay my hands on. I thought I was in Paradise."

A washing machine broke the routine of slavery as when all the work was done by hand. At Granny's farmhouse, long years before, the old kitchen held a great sandstone sink that had been worn by continual use. To the right of the sink stood a stone slopstone, a wringing machine with wooden rollers and a large table. In the corner was a set-pot, made not of pot but of iron and set in a stone base with space for the fire that, given time, would heat water that was conveyed in a large zinc bucket from a stone trough in the yard. It was Edith's job on a Sunday to fill the set-pot in readiness for the Monday wash.

Covering the set-pot was a large wooden lid. A piece of brush shank was kept at the side so that the clothes which were "boiled" in the pot could be lifted out without the operator being scalded. The first task in advance of the weekly wash was to put the clothes to soak in two wooden "dolly tubs" – one for cleaner clothes and the other for the dirty, workaday clothes. Cold water was added, the second-named having a dash of washing soda.

The fire under the set-pot was kindled early and the clothes taken out of the tubs and wrung out through the mangle. They were then immersed in the set-pot, in which the water was by now bubbling merrily. Soft green soap was added, also a couple of handfuls of washing soda, and the clothes were left to boil for twenty minutes, by which time they were clean.

Transferred into a tub of cold water, they were "possed" with a dolly-stick and any dirty parts scrubbed with a hard brush. Rinsed again, they were put through the mangle once or twice to remove any surplus water. The next stage was to place them in a clothes-basket in which they were carried outdoors to be hung up on lines and, hopefully, dried by sunshine and breeze.

Now the washing process was done at the touch of a switch. After a particularly good lamb sale, a brand new electric cooker arrived at Capna'. Edith baked every day. The children found that airtight tins in the kitchen were always full of Eccles cakes and rock buns.

The routine of preparing for the winter by laying in a big stock of coal and food began in November. Greens, of Gargrave, supplied Capna' with five tons of coal that had been delivered to them by canal. The vehicle used to move the coal was an old lorry.

When Robert decided that one Sunday afternoon in summer would be spent picnicking by Malham Tarn, they found themselves in the company of Mr and Mrs Nicholls, the schoolteachers from Settle, and Arthur Harrison. The Carr children paddled in shallow places. Where the water was comparatively deep they floated on old inner tubes. Suddenly, with alarm, it was realised that wind and wave were carrying little Mary across the Tarn. The Nicholls's confessed they could not swim. Neither could Robert. So Arthur Harrison swam after Mary and brought her safely back to land.

On another "rare occasion," Robert arranged to take the family to Malham in the Land Rover on a special day. The villagers had planned tea and sports to celebrate the Queen's coronation. The children from Capna' were shy in the presence of children from Malham, being accustomed to playing with the young folk from Langcliffe or Settle. Robert gruffly ordered them back into the Land Rover, drove them to the top of the hill and left them to walk back home, which they did tearfully, having missed both tea and sports. On the day of the Coronation, however, the family travelled to Lee Gate, where the latest acquisition was a television set. They joined the throng watching events in London on a nine-inch screen. The pictures were, of course, in black-and-white.

One Christmas, the special treat at Capna' was a television set. "Until the novelty wore off, we sat and watched everything that appeared on the screen. It was a real time-waster. About that time, the telephone arrived so we could natter away to each other in our own homes."

Shortly after Christmas each year, the farm folk were invited to a party held at Malham Tarn House. Mary Holmes decorated a huge tree. There was a present for each child who attended. Father Christmas distributed these gifts after tea.

Edith looked forward to attending the monthly meetings of Malham Women's Institute, though more than likely there was a crisis with stock or family on the day itself. At the WI she sat through cookery demonstrations and "make-up" sessions. "I usually tried out the unusual cookery on the family, not always meeting with their approval. The tried-and-tested recipes out of a tattered recipe book that had belonged to my Granny continued to be firm favourites."

There were happy days in Malham when the show was held and a proud Edith collected medals for her geraniums and fuschias. She was awarded a "gold medal" for needlework.

The women on Malham Moor had not had much of a social life, they were left at home while the men socialised down at Malham. "The men used to come to our house; they'd talk about their tups and yows. I used to get fed-up with all their talk. It was another sheep-meeting." The women did make a special effort to get to the Women's Institute. "We enjoyed each other's company when we got down there but in summer there were always jobs to do on the farm and our socialising ended on many a winter evening with the appearance of Willie Hudson, a local farmer. He kept an eye on the fickle weather. If conditions deteriorated, he would come round to 'Bessie's Hut' to report that snow was falling and 'you'd better be getting back on t'tops or else you'll nivver mak it'."

Edith and her neighbours quickly made haste. Husbands were collected from neighbouring houses or pubs. "Many is the struggle we had to get to the top of the Cove road, with its steep gradients and hairpin bends. The wheels of our vehicles spun on snow or ice. When we reached the exposed Moor, we were in the face of a full-blown blizzard. I was always thankful to turn in along the farm lane. Half-frozen, we mustered enough strength for a large pot of strong tea and a bite to eat. When we had thawed out we could face the bedroom, with its icy sheets and floors covered with chilling oilcloth."

The mid-1950s are remembered as a time when all the young stock was lost through an anthrax scare. When a stirk went down, it was considered a normal loss, but then piglets and more cattle were found dead and the specialist arrived to investigate. They decided it was anthrax and the Carr family sorrowfully watched as a great pit was dug for the dead stock. The pit was sealed with lime.

Once only, during the spell at Capna', did the Carr family see the spectacle of the Northern Lights. It was at the back-end of the year, at a time of clear, frosty weather. They stared with astonishment at a rainbow-hued display in the heavens.

Epilogue

NOWT'S SAME – not even the weather. "Rain, snow and frost – you got everything really bad. It didn't just come a scattering of snow; it was deep! It's a different climate and a different world. It's not Malham Moor as it used to be."

Remember, says Edith, that this was a time when hill farmers sank or swam. They had no government grants or subsidies. They had a pride in their work. Robert was a good waller and a hard master if anyone else had a go at the drystone walls at Capna'. "If some gap-walling was not done right, he'd knock it down and tell whoever had done it to start again. He did that with our Robin, who used to say he was fed up with his dad, for there was nowt wrong with the wall.

"I would say: 'Just put up with it, Robin, and it'll pay off'. And it did pay off. When Robin was 15 years of age, a friend invited him to go with him to a drystone walling competition at Gatehouse of Fleet. Unbeknown to us, he entered, being the youngest competitor, and came home with the gold medal. We were immensely proud of him."

In 1965, Edith and Robert received a letter stating that Capna' was to be sold because the owners of Langcliffe Mills were closing them down. All the money had to be called in to pay creditors. The Trust accepted the highest price to be offered which, alas, was not from Edith and Robert. "We had to move out." Their new home, at Langcliffe, was about the same size as their first home had been. It was decked with furnishings and pictures that reminded them of a quarter of a century of struggle at the old spot on Malham Moor.

Robert never quite settled in to life in the lowlands. Edith kept a few sheep that were more like pets than a serious commercial project. When she was working among the sheep, she wore the woollen cap that had belonged to Robert. And, as related, she would glance at the hills where Robert's ashes were scattered. She spent part of every day in her unique pavement garden at Langcliffe.

Now she has a bungalow on a trim Council estate at Settle. What had been a modest garden has blossomed into a floral showpiece. Edith busies herself with a Millennium tapestry. Quite often, her mind strays to thoughts of Capna', on the Pennine skyline. "When I think back now, I don't know how I stuck it. But when you've a family you've to just keep going."

Edith was thinking nostalgically of Capna' when she wrote:

High upon the hilltop, clear for all to see,
Stands a grey and lonely house that once was home to me.
Gone is the limestone cobbled yard, I weeded with such care
Lest lichen grey or mossy green should find a refuge there.
The old oak door is modernised, no gleaming knocker there.
No flower-filled basket – hanging overhead,
No fern-filled tub – standing near.

Gone is the little garden patch where jonquils grew so far.
No gurgling baby in his pram, no children playing there.
No sheepdog barking in the yard; no cattle – anywhere.
No Julia, Mary, Chris and Ann, neighbours gathered there for tea.
Just loneliness there – that is all I could see.

I enter now my dear old home, yet sad am I to be.
'Tis not for me, this shining scheme of cold-looking stainless steel.
Give me bright pictures on the wall, clean washing there to see;
A kettle boiling on the hob, with kindling lying near,
A brightly-coloured home-pegged rug, a kitten snoozing there;
A sofa wide with cushions red, beside an old armchair,
A gleaming cloth, laid there for tea – children calling me:
"Mam! Where are you Mam? Are you there?"
That is home to me.

Died Spring 2007,